MW01594896

Fast And Easy Cauliflower Recipes

Table of contents

Introduction

Cauliflower is type of vegetable that fits in that group of veggies we rarely consume. Although this wonderful veggie has many positive health benefits, we most often forget about it because we do not have too many ideas on how to prepare it.

This eBook is solution for this type of problem. You can find here great ideas, for breakfast, lunch and dinner meals, that are easy to make but are highly delicious.

25 best recipes that will satisfy even the most demanding gourmet will definitely find its way to your table too and present you the cauliflower in the best possible way.

If you still do not believe in all we are saying about cauliflower, let us introduce you to the cauliflower positive effects on our organism.

Cauliflower health benefits

- Nutritional: Cauliflower is nutritional vegetable, which contains vitamins B1, B2, B3, B5 and B9 also known as folic acid. It also contains vitamin K and omega 3-fatty acids. Cauliflower is valuable source of manganese, vitamin C, which are powerful antioxidants.

- Antioxidation: Besides these antioxidants listed above, cauliflower also contains carotenoids such as beta-carotene and phytonutrients that include ferulic acid, cinnamic and caffeic acid. With these antioxidants, cauliflower will protect you from all those free-radicals and reduce your risks for diseases caused by them.

- Detoxification: Cauliflower also contains glucosinolates and thiocyanates, which help to increase the liver's ability to neutralise potentially toxic substances that could lead to cancer if left unattended and also help in detoxifying process.

- Anti-Inflammatory: According to some studies, cauliflower consumption can help decrease the risk of inflammation-mediated diseases such as arthritis, obesity, diabetes mellitus, inflammatory bowel disease and ulcerative colitis. Just one cup of boiled cauliflower contains about 11 micrograms of vitamin K and 0.21 g omega-3 fatty acids. Because of the omega-3 fatty acids and vitamin K in cauliflower, it helps to prevent chronic inflammation that leads to conditions such as arthritis, chronic pain, and certain bowel conditions.

- Digestive support: Like most of vegetables, cauliflower is valuable source of dietary fibers which helps clean your digestive system and gets rid of unnecessary substances. Additionally, a substance called glucoraphin present in cauliflower appears to have a protective effect on stomach lining. With glucoraphin, your stomach is not prone to the bacterium helicobacter pylori, thereby reducing your risk for stomach ulcer and cancer.

As you can see in the final, cauliflower is more than just a simple vegetable. With regular consumption you can really experience all of it positive effects and much more.

Some nutritional facts about cauliflower:

- The good: This food is very low in Saturated Fat and Cholesterol. It is also a good source of Protein, Thiamin, Riboflavin, Niacin, Magnesium and Phosphorus, and a very good source of Dietary Fiber, Vitamin C, Vitamin K, Vitamin B6, Folate, Pantothenic Acid, Potassium and Manganese.

- The bad: A large portion of the calories in this food come from sugars.

Breakfast ideas
Breakfast cauliflower pancakes

Serves: 4

Ingredients:

- 2 cups cauliflower, chopped
- 4 large eggs, room temperature
- 1 cup onion, diced
- ¼ teaspoon salt
- ¼ teaspoon black pepper
- ¼ cup diced spring onions
- ¼ cup breadcrumbs
- 1 cup shredded cheddar cheese
- Some vegetable oil – to fry

Preparation method:

1. Bring salted water to boil in medium sized pot and add cauliflower; cook for 8-10 minutes or until tender.
2. Drain and mash the cauliflower while is still warm.
3. Add shredded cheese, whisked eggs, spring onion spices and breadcrumbs.
4. Stir well until combined thoroughly.
5. Coat the non-stick skillet with some oil and heat over medium-high heat.
6. Add prepared mixture to skillet and swirl to get a kind of pancake and flatten with spatula.
7. Cook for 3-4 minutes, each side, or until golden-brown.
8. Serve while still hot.

Nutritional Analysis:

Good points:

- High in calcium
- Very high in vitamin B6

- High in vitamin C

Bad points:

- High in saturated fat
- High in sodium

Cauliflower with scrambled eggs

Serves: 2

Ingredients:

- 1 cup cauliflower, chopped
- 4 eggs, slightly whisked
- 2 teaspoons butter
- Fresh ground salt and pepper
- 1 tablespoon chives

Preparation method:

1. Heat the skillet over medium-high heat.
2. Whisk the eggs with salt and pepper, add chives and cauliflower; stir to combine.
3. Add butter to the skillet and when melted add cauliflower mixture;
4. Cook for 5-7 minutes, stirring in the pan or until the eggs are set.
5. Serve immediately with some toasted bread.

Nutritional Analysis:

Good points:

- High in pantothenic acid
- High in phosphorus
- High in riboflavin
- High in selenium
- High in vitamin B6
- Very high in vitamin C

Bad points:

- High in saturated fat
- Very high in cholesterol

Breakfast cauliflower skillet

Serves: 4

Ingredients:

- 2 cups cauliflower, grated or processed in food processor
- 2 eggs
- 1 tablespoon olive oil
- 3 bacon strips, cooked and crumbled
- 1 tablespoon ghee
- 1 cup shredded parmesan
- 3 spring onions, chopped
- 1 carrot, grated
- 4 egg whites
- Fresh ground salt and pepper
- 1 teaspoon hot sauce

Preparation method:

1. Place oven rack to middle slot and preheat the broiler.
2. Heat ghee and olive oil in oven-proof skillet over medium-high heat.
3. Add carrot, cauliflower and season with salt and pepper. Cook for 7 minutes or until the veggies are tender.
4. Whisk the eggs, egg whites, ½ cheese, spring onions, hot sauce, bacon, salt and pepper in a large bowl.
5. When veggies are cooked, spread them evenly on the bottom of skillet in single layer; pour over egg mixture and smooth the top with spatula.
6. Cook for 3-4 minutes or until the sides are set and sprinkle with remaining cheese.
7. Set under broiler and cook for 4-5 minutes or until cheese is bubbly.
8. Remove the skillet from the oven and let it rest for 10 minutes before slicing.
9. Slice and garnish with some chopped onions before serving.

Nutritional Analysis:

Good points:

- Very high in vitamin B6
- Very high in vitamin C

Bad points:

- High in saturated fat

Cauliflower bacon hash

Serves: 4

Ingredients:

- 6 slices bacon, diced
- ¾ lb. cauliflower
- ½ cup yellow onion, chopped
- ½ teaspoon smoked paprika
- 2 garlic cloves, minced
- 2 teaspoons butter
- Fresh ground salt and pepper
- 3 tablespoons water
- Juice of ½ lemon
- 4 eggs, hardboiled

Preparation method:

1. Cook the bacon in medium sized skillet over medium-high heat for 8-10 minutes or until crispy.
2. Remove the bacon on kitchen towel, but reserve the fat.
3. In the same skillet cook cauliflower, onion and garlic for 3 minutes or until starts to golden.
4. Season with salt and pepper and add smoked paprika, stir to combine.
5. Add water and cover the skillet with lid; cook further for 5 minutes.
6. Return bacon to the skillet and add lemon juice.
7. Cook for 2 minutes more and remove from the heat.
8. Serve with halved hardboiled eggs while still hot.

Nutritional Analysis:

Good points:

- Very high in dietary fiber
- High in manganese
- High in vitamin A

- Very high in vitamin B6
- Very high in vitamin C

Bad points:

- Very high in cholesterol

Cauliflower stakes with kale and poached eggs

Serves: 4

Ingredients:

- ½ cauliflower head
- 5 cups raw kale, chopped
- 4 garlic cloves, minced
- 4 eggs
- Salt and pepper – to taste
- 2 tablespoons olive oil

Preparation method:

1. Cut cauliflower in steaks, by length, 1-inch thick.
2. Season each side with salt and pepper.
3. Heat 1 tablespoon of olive oil in a large skillet; add cauliflower steaks and cook for 2 minutes, each side or until golden.
4. Poach the eggs; fill a sauce pan with water and bring to boil.
5. Add salt and reduce heat so water boils low or simmer.
6. Crack egg in small bowl and gently slide in water; cook for 45 seconds and remove with slotted spoon.
7. Repeat the process with remaining eggs.
8. In a separate skillet heat remaining oil and add garlic; cook for 1 minute or until very fragrant.
9. Add chopped kale and cook until wilted and remove from the heat.
10. Serve kale in large plate, top with cauliflower and top all with poached eggs.

Nutritional Analysis:

Good points:

- High in dietary fiber
- High in manganese
- High in potassium
- Very high in vitamin A

- High in vitamin B6
- Very high in vitamin C

Cauliflower fritters

Serves: 4

Ingredients:

- 4 cups cauliflower, chopped
- 2 garlic cloves, minced
- ¼ cup grated cheese – by your choice
- 1 egg, whisked
- 3 tablespoons hot water
- 2 tablespoons olive oil
- Fresh ground salt and pepper
- 2 tablespoons flat-leaf parsley, chopped
- ½ cup whole wheat flour

Preparation method:

1. Cook the cauliflower in 2 cups water, for 6-7 minutes or until tender.
2. Drain well and rinse in cold water, to stop the cooking.
3. Chop the cauliflower and set in a bowl.
4. Add slightly whisked egg, parsley, fresh ground salt and pepper, flour, garlic and grated cheese.
5. Add water and stir to combine. If needed add more water to have mixture slightly more dense than pancake batter.
6. Heat large non-stick skillet over medium-high heat and coat the pan with some oil.
7. Place 4 fritters in the pan and cook for 2-3 minutes per side or until golden.
8. Repeat the process until you have no mixture left.
9. Serve while still hot.

Nutritional Analysis:

Good points:

- Very low in sodium
- Low in sugar

- High in selenium
- High in thiamin

Cauliflower and sausage bake

Serves: 4

Ingredients:

- 6 pork sausages
- 3 cups cauliflower, cut into florets
- 8 rashers bacon, cooked and crumbled
- 1 ½ cup grated cheese, by your choice
- 4 tablespoons butter
- 4 tablespoons all-purpose flour
- 2 tablespoons milk
- Fresh ground salt – to taste

Preparation method:

1. Preheat oven to 200C/400F.
2. Place sausages in baking dish and bake for 30 minutes; set aside to cool slightly and slice.
3. Steam cauliflower for 2o minutes or until tender and set aside.
4. Place butter in a sauce pan and heat over medium heat; when melted add flour and stir to combine.
5. Whisk in the milk and simmer, until you have creamy mixture.
6. Stir in ½ cup cheese and set aside.
7. In a baking dish add cauliflower, sliced sausage and bacon.
8. Pour over the prepared cheese mixture and sprinkle over with remaining cheese.
9. Bake for 30 minutes and set on wire rack to cool.
10. Serve while still hot.

Nutritional Analysis:

Good points:

- High in vitamin B6
- Very high in vitamin C

Bad points:

- Very high in saturated fat

Lunch ideas
Cauliflower with herbs

Serves:

Ingredients:

- 1 cauliflower head, cut into florets
- 1 tablespoon olive oil
- ½ tablespoon chopped flat-leaf parsley
- 1 teaspoon chopped thyme
- 1 teaspoon fresh tarragon, chopped
- 2 garlic cloves, minced
- ½ oz. grated Parmesan
- Fresh ground salt and pepper
- 1 tablespoon lemon juice

Preparation method:

1. Preheat oven to 220C/450F.
2. Place cauliflower in baking pan and drizzle with olive oil.
3. Toss well to coat evenly and bake for 20 minutes, stirring each 5-7 minutes.
4. Sprinkle with herbs and garlic. Toss once again to combine and bake for 5 minutes.
5. Combine cauliflower with Parmesan cheese and toss to combine.
6. Let it rest for 5 minutes before serving.

Nutritional Analysis:

Good points:

- High in calcium
- High in phosphorus
- High in vitamin B6
- Very high in vitamin C

Bad points:

- High in saturated fat

Cauliflower curry rice with meatballs

Serves: 4

Ingredients:

- 14 oz. minced pork
- 1 onion, finely chopped
- 1 egg
- 2 garlic cloves, minced
- 1 teaspoon salt
- ½ teaspoon ground chili

Curry:

- 1 can coconut milk, full fat
- ½ cup chicken stock
- 2 cups onions, chopped
- 2 garlic cloves, minced
- 4 carrots, grated
- 1 teaspoon grated ginger
- 1 tablespoon curry
- 1 teaspoon ground cumin
- 1 teaspoon salt
- 2 tablespoon yellow curry paste
- ½ teaspoon chili flakes
- ½ tablespoon butter

Cauliflower rice:

- 1 cauliflower head
- 1 tablespoon parsley

Preparation method:

1. The meatballs; combine all ingredients in a bowl using fingers until you have well combined mixture.
2. Cover with plastic foil and set in the refrigerator until ready to use.

3. The curry; melt butter and add onions and garlic; cook for couple minutes.
4. Add curry paste and curry powder; let it get some heat to release flavors.
5. Add carrots, coconut milk and chicken stock.
6. Reduce heat to medium and let it simmer for 30 minutes.
7. Meanwhile fill the pot with water and season with salt and remove the meat from the fridge.
8. When water starts to boil scoop the balls with metal spoon and set in boiling water, one after other.
9. When balls start to swim on surface they are cooked and remove them with slotted spoon.
10. The cauliflower rice; process the cauliflower florets in food processor until you have structure similar to rice.
11. Place the rice in a bowl and pour over with boiling water, let it stand for 5 minutes and the rice is prepared.
12. Serve rice in a large plate, top with meatballs and pour over curry sauce.

Nutritional Analysis:

Good points:

- High in dietary fiber
- Very high in vitamin B6
- Very high in vitamin C

Bad points:

- High in cholesterol
- Very high in sodium

Cauliflower casserole

Serves: 4

Ingredients:

- 2 medium cauliflower heads, cut into florets
- 5 oz. sour cream
- 2 ½ oz. shredded cheddar cheese
- ¼ cup chopped green pepper
- ¼ cup chopped red pepper
- 1/3 cup crushed cornflakes
- ¼ cup grated Parmesan
- Dash of smoked paprika
- Fresh ground salt and pepper – to taste

Preparation method:

1. Preheat oven to 160C/325F.
2. Place cauliflower in sauce pan and pour over small amount of water, around ¼ cup.
3. Cover and cook for 5 minutes; drain well and set aside.
4. In a bowl, combine cauliflower, salt and pepper, cornflakes, peppers and cheddar cheese.
5. Transfer to slightly grease baking pan and sprinkle with Parmesan and smoked paprika.
6. Bake, uncovered for 30-35 minutes.
7. Serve while still hot.

Nutritional Analysis:

Good points:

- Low in sodium
- High in dietary fiber
- High in potassium
- Very high in vitamin A
- Very high in vitamin B6
- Very high in vitamin C

Bad points:

- High in saturated fat
- High in sugar

Cauliflower and potato curry

Serves: 4

Ingredients:

- 1 cauliflower head, cut into florets
- 2 potatoes, diced
- 2 tablespoons olive oil
- 1 cup onion, chopped
- 3 garlic cloves, minced
- 1 teaspoon cumin
- ½ teaspoon turmeric
- 1 teaspoon mild curry powder
- 12 oz. can crushed tomatoes
- ½ teaspoon sugar
- 1 jalapeno pepper, chopped
- 1 teaspoon lemon juice

Preparation method:

1. Heat olive oil in medium sized sauce pan.
2. When hot add onion and cook for 10 minutes. Add turmeric, curry, cumin and garlic; cook for 1 minute or until very fragrant over medium-high heat.
3. Stir in the crushed tomatoes and sugar.
4. Add jalapeno peppers, potatoes and cauliflower; stir to combine.
5. Cover and reduce heat to medium; simmer for 30 minutes.
6. Whet the vegetables are tender add lemon juice and stir to combine.
7. Serve while still hot.

Nutritional Analysis:

Good points:

- No cholesterol
- Low in sodium

- High in dietary fiber
- High in potassium
- Very high in vitamin B6
- Very high in vitamin C

Bad points:

- High in sugar

Cauliflower and anchovy pasta

Serves: 4

Ingredients:

- 1 cauliflower head
- ¼ cup + 2 tablespoons vegetable oil
- 1 lb. penne pasta
- 4 garlic cloves, minced
- 4 anchovy fillets, drained
- ¾ cup breadcrumbs
- ¼ cup chopped parsley
- ½ cup grated Parmesan
- 1 jalapeno pepper, deseeded
- Fresh ground salt and pepper

Preparation method:

1. Preheat oven to 200C/400F and line baking tray with parchment paper.
2. Wash cauliflower and cut in ½-inch slices.
3. Transfer to a large bowl and drizzle over with 2 tablespoons vegetable oil; season with salt and pepper and toss to coat well.
4. Set the cauliflower onto baking sheet and bake for 20-25 minutes, turning half way through.
5. Remove from the oven and set aside.
6. Prepare penne pasta according to package instruction and set aside. Reserve 1 cup of pasta water.
7. Meanwhile prepare the sauce; heat remaining oil in medium-sized sauce pan over medium-high heat.
8. Add garlic and cook for 1 minute. Add jalapeno pepper and continue cooking for 1 minute more.
9. Add anchovies and cook for 2 minutes or until anchovies are dissolved.
10. Gently stir the cauliflower and remove from the heat.

11. Combine prepared cauliflower with cooked pasta, breadcrumbs, Parmesan cheese, pasta water and toss to combine; serve while still hot.

Nutritional Analysis:

Good points:

- Low in saturated fat
- Low in sugar
- High in thiamin
- High in vitamin C

Cauliflower soup

Serves: 4

Ingredients:

- 1 cauliflower head, cut into florets
- 4 cups chicken stock
- 1 lb. potatoes, peeled and diced
- ½ cup sour cream
- 2 garlic cloves, crushed
- ½ teaspoon cumin
- 1 cup yellow onion, diced
- 1 tablespoon olive oil
- Fresh ground pepper

Preparation method:

1. Heat olive oil in large sauce pan over medium-high heat.
2. Add onion and garlic; cook for 3-5 minutes or until soften.
3. Add potatoes and cauliflower florets; cook, stirring occasionally for 5-6 minutes.
4. Add stock and season with pepper.
5. Cover the sauce pan and bring to boil; reduce heat to medium and simmer for 18-20 minutes or until potatoes are tender.
6. Set aside to cool and using hand blender, blend in batches until smooth.
7. Add sour cream and stir to combine; cook for 2 minutes more and serve with bread croutons on top.

Nutritional Analysis:

Good points:

- Very high in vitamin B6
- Very high in vitamin C

Bad points:

- High in saturated fat

Cauliflower and bacon gratin

Serves: 4

Ingredients:

- 1 cauliflower head, cut into florets
- 1 tablespoon butter
- ¼ cup plain flour
- 1 ½ cup milk
- ¼ cup grated cheddar
- Fresh ground salt and pepper
- 3.5 oz. bacon

Preparation method:

1. Preheat oven to 200C/400F.
2. Cook cauliflower in large pot of salted boiling water for 8-10 minutes.
3. Drain well and set aside.
4. Heat medium non-stick skillet over medium high heat and add bacon; cook for 5-6 minutes or until crisp.
5. Set on plate lined with kitchen towel.
6. Melt the butter in small sauce pan and add flour; cook for 30 seconds and gradually add half of the milk, whisking to combine.
7. Add the remaining milk and continue cooking for 5 minutes or until sauce thickens.
8. Stir in the cheese and season with salt and pepper.
9. Arrange cauliflower in baking dish and top with half of the bacon and cheddar cheese sauce; finish with remaining bacon and bake for 15 minutes.
10. Serve while still hot.

Nutritional Analysis:

Good points:

- Low in sugar

- High in selenium
- Very high in vitamin C

Cauliflower and mint couscous

Serves: 4

Ingredients:

- 2 cups cauliflower, cut into florets
- ¼ cup chopped mint
- ¼ cup chopped parsley
- 1 cup crumbled feta
- 2 ½ cups couscous
- Grated zest of 1 lemon
- ½ cup pine nuts, toasted
- 1/3 cup olive oil

Preparation method:

1. Cook cauliflower in a sauce pan of boiling, salted water for 1 minute. Drain well.
2. Bring 3 ½ cups of water, salt and oil to boil in sauce pan.
3. Stir couscous and cover with lid. Let it stand for 10 minutes.
4. Place couscous, cauliflower, crumbled feta, pine nuts and lemon zest in a large bowl. Add herbs.
5. Toss to combine and serve immediately.

Nutritional Analysis:

Good points:

- Low in cholesterol
- Low in sodium
- Low in sugar
- High in manganese

Cauliflower pizza

Serves: 6

Ingredients:

- ½ cauliflower head, coarsely chopped
- 1 egg
- 1 teaspoon chopped garlic
- Fresh ground salt and pepper
- ½ cup shredded Parmesan
- 2 tablespoons chopped basil
- 1 cup marinara sauce
- 4 slices mozzarella cheese

Preparation method:

1. Place cauliflower pieces in food processor and pulse until shredded finely.
2. Set cauliflower in in pan and fill the bottom with water; cover and steam for 15 minutes.
3. Set aside to cool.
4. Preheat oven to 220C/450F and line baking tray with parchment paper.
5. Combine parmesan, egg, garlic, salt and pepper until evenly combined.
6. Press and shape into pizza crust and bake for 10 minutes.
7. Remove from the oven and top with marinara sauce, mozzarella and basil.
8. Bake further for 5-8 minutes or until cheese is melted.

Nutritional Analysis:

Good points:

- High in dietary fiber
- High in niacin
- High in potassium
- High in vitamin B6

- Very high in vitamin C

Bad points:

- High in sodium
- High in sugar

Dinner ideas
Cauliflower steaks

Serves: 4

Ingredients:

- 1 cauliflower head, cut in ½-inch thick slices
- ½ cup green olives, chopped
- 3 sundried tomatoes, sliced
- 3 tablespoons olive oil, divided
- 3 tablespoons parsley, chopped
- 2 tomatoes, cored and quartered
- Fresh ground salt and pepper
- 2 garlic cloves, minced

Preparation method:

1. Preheat oven to 200C/400F.
2. Heat 1 ½ tablespoon olive oil in large skillet; cook cauliflower steaks until golden brown.
3. Transfer steaks to the large baking sheet and bake in the oven for 15 minutes.
4. Return skillet over medium-high heat and add garlic and fresh tomatoes.
5. Cook until browned and set the skillet in oven; bake for 10-12 minutes.
6. Transfer the tomatoes, sun dried tomatoes and garlic in food processor; add olive oil and olives; pulse until smooth.
7. Serve cauliflower steaks and top each with prepared tomato sauce.

Nutritional Analysis:

Good points:

- No cholesterol
- Low in sodium
- High in dietary fiber

- High in potassium
- High in vitamin A
- High in vitamin B6
- Very high in vitamin C

Bad points:

- High in sugar

Cauliflower-Parmesan mash with chicken sticks

Serves: 4

Ingredients:

For the cauliflower mash:

- 1 cauliflower head, cut into florets
- 1 cup chicken stock
- 2 garlic cloves, minced
- 1/3 cup yogurt, thick
- Fresh ground salt and pepper
- 2 tablespoons Parmesan cheese, grated

Chicken sticks:

- 1 ½ lb. chicken breasts, cut into strips
- 1 teaspoon smoked paprika
- Fresh ground salt and pepper
- 1 tablespoon olive oil

Preparation method:

1. Cauliflower mash; in a large sauce pan bring chicken stock, garlic and cauliflower to boil.
2. Reduce heat to low, and simmer for 20 minutes or until cauliflower is tender.
3. Pour the excess stock and set the cauliflower in food processor, with the garlic.
4. Add remaining ingredients and pulse in food processor until smooth.
5. Set aside and prepare the chicken sticks; cut the chicken breasts in ½-inch thick stripes.
6. Season with salt and pepper and sprinkle with smoked paprika.
7. Heat olive oil in large non-stick skillet and cook the chicken until golden, for 7-9 minutes.
8. Serve cauliflower mash with chicken while still warm.

Nutritional Analysis:

Good points:

- Low in cholesterol
- High in calcium
- High in phosphorus
- High in potassium
- High in vitamin B6
- Very high in vitamin C

Bad points:

- High in sodium

Cauliflower with fish

Serves:

Ingredients:

- 1 lb. cauliflower, cut into florets
- Fresh ground salt and pepper
- 2 ½ cups milk
- 1 cup onion, chopped
- 1 celery rib
- ½ lb. tilapia fillets
- 1 tablespoon dill weed, chopped
- 4 slices bread, torn into pieces
- 2 tablespoons olive oil
- 1 large carrot, diced

Preparation method:

1. Preheat oven to 220C/450F.
2. Place milk and cauliflower in sauce pan and bring to boil over medium high heat.
3. Bring to low simmer, and cook for 5-7 minutes.
4. Remove cauliflower and reserve milk.
5. Place cauliflower in food processor and pulse until smooth.
6. Add some of the reserved milk if needed and season with salt and pepper.
7. Heat half of olive oil non-stick skillet and cook onion for 2 minutes.
8. Add celery, carrot and cook further for 5 minutes.
9. Season with salt and pepper and add fish and cauliflower mash.
10. Transfer all in baking dish; toss bread with remaining oil and top the cauliflower mixture with bread.
11. Bake for 20 minutes or until bread is golden.
12. Serve while still warm.

Nutritional Analysis:

Good points:

- Very high in vitamin B6
- Very high in vitamin C

Bad points:

- High in cholesterol

Spanish crisp cauliflower

Serves: 2

Ingredients:

- 1 teaspoon smoked paprika
- ½ cauliflower heat, cut into florets
- 2 tablespoons gram flour
- 1 tablespoon red wine vinegar
- 1 tablespoon caper, rinsed and chopped
- 1 tablespoon chopped flat-leaf parsley
- Fresh ground salt and pepper
- Some vegetable oil- to fry

Preparation method:

1. Cook the cauliflower in pot of salted boiling water, until just tender, for 10 minutes.
2. Drain well and while still hot set in a large bowl; season with salt and pepper, paprika and add flour.
3. Toss to coat the cauliflower well.
4. Heat the vegetable oil until starts to simmer.
5. Fry the cauliflower on batches until crisp and golden.
6. Set in a large bowl, sprinkle with capers, vinegar and chopped parsley; toss to combine.
7. Serve while still warm.

Nutritional Analysis:

Good points

- Low in saturated fat
- No cholesterol
- Very high in dietary fiber
- High in iron
- High in manganese
- High in magnesium
- High in potassium

- Very high in vitamin A
- High in vitamin B6
- Very high in vitamin C

Bad points:

- Very high in sodium

Cauliflower and quinoa cakes

Serves: 4

Ingredients:

- 4 eggs
- 1 ½ cups cauliflower florets
- 1 cup quinoa, cooked
- 4 scallions, chopped
- 1 1/3 cup feta cheese, crumbled
- Zest of 1 lemon
- ½ cup chopped parsley
- Fresh ground salt and pepper
- 1 teaspoon dried basil
- Some vegetable oil – to fry

Preparation method:

1. Place cauliflower in food processor and process until you have similar to rice pieces.
2. Place cauliflower in a bowl and add remaining ingredients.
3. Stir ingredients with hands, until well combined.
4. Heat vegetable oil in large non-stick skillet and form cakes from the prepared mixture.
5. Cook the cakes, 4 minutes per side, or until golden brown.
6. Serve immediately.

Nutritional Analysis:

Good points:

- Low in saturated fat
- Very low in sodium
- Very low in sugar
- High in manganese
- High in magnesium
- High in phosphorus
- High in vitamin A

- Very high in vitamin C

Cauliflower savory tart

Serves: 6

Ingredients:

For the crust:

- ½ cup toasted walnuts
- ½ cup rolled oats
- ½ teaspoon baking soda
- Fresh ground salt and pepper
- 1 cup whole wheat flour
- 2 tablespoons milk
- 2 tablespoons olive oil

For the filling:

- 2 tablespoons extra virgin olive oil
- 4 garlic cloves, minced
- 3 tablespoons lemon juice
- ¼ cup almond milk
- 2 cups onions, chopped
- Fresh ground salt and pepper

Cauliflower:

- 2 lb. cauliflower, cut into florets
- ½ teaspoon salt
- 2 tablespoons olive oil

Preparation method:

1. Preheat oven to 200C/400F and line baking tray with parchment paper.
2. Combine olive oil, cauliflower and salt in a bowl. Spread onto baking tray and bake for 30 minutes, turning after 15 minutes, so they evenly roast. Set aside.
3. Prepare the crust; oil 9-inch tart pan and reduce oven heat to 180C/350F.

4. Place walnuts, baking soda, salt, pepper and oats in food processor; pulse until well combined.
5. Transfer to the bowl and add whole wheat flour; stir to combine.
6. Add remaining crust ingredients and stir until well blended. Press the prepared dough into greased pan, distributing evenly.
7. Prick the crust with a fork and bake for 15 minutes. Set on wire rack and prepare the filling.
8. Heat oil in non-stick skillet and onions; cook until lightly brown. Add garlic and cook for 5 minutes more. Reduce heat and continue cooking or until onion is caramelized.
9. Set in the food processor and add cauliflower, milk, lemon juice and season with pepper.
10. Pulse until smooth and transfer into baked tart shell.
11. Bake tart for 30 minutes and set on wire rack to cool.
12. Slice before serving.

Nutritional Analysis:

Good points:

- Very low in cholesterol
- High in manganese
- Very high in vitamin B6
- High in vitamin C

Bad points:

- High in saturated fat

Roasted cauliflower and yogurt salad

Serves: 4

Ingredients:

- ½ cauliflower head
- ½ tablespoon cumin
- 1 celery stalk, chopped
- 2 garlic cloves, minced
- 2 tablespoons crushed walnuts
- ¼ cup spring onion
- ½ cup yogurt
- ½ lemon, juice and zest
- Fresh ground salt and pepper
- 2 tablespoons olive oil
- 2 tablespoons fresh coriander

Preparation method:

1. Preheat oven to 200C/400F and line baking tray with parchment paper.
2. Cut cauliflower in florets and set in a bowl; add 1 tablespoon olive oil, cumin, garlic and season with salt and pepper; toss to combine and spread onto baking sheet.
3. Bake for 15 minutes and set on wire rack.
4. Meanwhile combine chopped celery, spring onion and walnuts in a bowl. Add yogurt, lemon zest and juice and remaining olive oil; stir to combine.
5. Add cauliflower, toss to coat and serve in small bowls: garnish with chopped coriander before serving.

Nutritional Analysis:

Good points:

- Low in cholesterol
- High in calcium
- High in phosphorus

- High in potassium

Cauliflower casserole with cashew sauce

Serves: 4

Ingredients:

- 1 1/3 cauliflower head, cut into florets
- 2/3 cup raw cashews
- 2/3 cup potato mash
- 1 teaspoon minced garlic
- 1 1/3 cups chicken stock
- 2 teaspoons Dijon mustard
- 2 teaspoons tomato paste
- 1 1/3 teaspoon smoked paprika
- 2 ½ tablespoons olive oil
- 1/3 cup frozen peas
- Fresh ground salt and pepper

Preparation method:

1. Preheat oven to 200C/400F.
2. Bring stock and cashews to boil and blend using hand blender until smooth.
3. Add garlic, potato puree, tomato paste, mustard, smoked paprika, 1 teaspoon olive oil and salt.
4. Combine cauliflower with remaining oil and season with salt and pepper.
5. Roast in single layer onto baking tray, lined with parchment paper for 25 minutes.
6. In a casserole dish combine peas, roasted cauliflower and prepared sauce; stir to combine and bake for 20 minutes more.
7. Serve while still hot.

Nutritional Analysis:

Good points:

- No cholesterol
- Low in sodium

- High in magnesium

Cauliflower and onion quiche

Serves: 4

Ingredients:

The crust:

- 12 oz. all-purpose flour
- 6 tablespoons ice cold water
- Dash of salt
- 6 oz. cold butter, diced

Quiche filling:

- ½ head cauliflower
- 1 brow onion, diced
- 1 cup grated cheese, like Gruyere
- ½ cup grated parmesan cheese
- 4 eggs
- 1 cup heavy cream
- 2 teaspoons Dijon mustard

Preparation method:

1. Combine flour and salt in food processor; add cubed butter and pulse until you have coarse meal mixture.
2. Add water and pulse until you have smooth dough.
3. Transfer dough onto plastic foil, shape it in the disc and wrap in the foil, refrigerate for 30 minutes.
4. Roll out the dough on slightly floured kitchen surface to ¼-inch thick. Transfer into pie dish and bake for 25.-30 minutes; set on wire rack.
5. Prepare the filling; combine cauliflower florets with olive oil and season with salt and pepper.
6. Roast in oven on baking tray, lined with parchment paper for 20 minutes. Set on wire rack to cool.
7. Caramelize onions on low heat for 20 minutes and combine with heavy cream.

8. Add eggs and cheese, reserving some of the Parmesan cheese.
9. Spread mustard over prepared crust; add caramelized onion with heavy cream, roasted cauliflower and pour over egg mixture.
10. Top with reserved Parmesan and bake for 45 minutes at 150C/250F
11. Serve while still hot.

Nutritional Analysis:

Good points:

- Low in sugar
- High in vitamin C

Bad points:

- Very high in saturated fat

29193733R00031

Made in the USA
Lexington, KY
26 January 2019